T0193430

GIRL TALK, MONEY TALK

The Smart Girl's Guide to Money After College

Lisa L. Brown, CFP®, CIMA®, MBA

authorHOUSE®

AuthorHouse™
1663 Liberty Drive
Bloomington, IN 47403
www.authorhouse.com
Phone: 1 (800) 839-8640

Published by AuthorHouse 07/08/2019

ISBN: 978-1-7283-1378-8 (sc)
ISBN: 978-1-7283-1377-1 (hc)
ISBN: 978-1-7283-1376-4 (e)

Library of Congress Control Number: 2019906335

Print information available on the last page.

ACKNOWLEDGEMENTS

With much love to my Editor-in-Chief and my #1 fan in life, JTBCNY.

The motivation and inspiration in all I do, CTB, IEB, SLB - my heart grows bigger every day for you.

To Mom and Dad, J&J – the best part of my first half!

PREFACE

Why This Book Matters and How It Will Help You

Before you begin to uncover the secrets to financial success in your twenties and thirties, and determine which stumbling blocks to avoid, I want to share with you why I wrote this book. While I enjoy writing and have been published numerous times in prestigious publications like the *New York Times*, the *Wall Street Journal*, Yahoo! Finance, Kiplinger, and others, I didn't have a desire to write an entire book until a few years ago.

I started seeing a concerning trend of women in their forties and fifties completely frozen, paralyzed even, from making any financial decision. The reason is that they were never taught basic money management lessons and had been content allowing Daddy and then Husband handle the financial matters up to this point. Here's how this played out:

I've been a financial advisor for twenty years, and most of my new clients come to me by word of mouth. I started getting a large number of phone calls from single women in their forties and fifties who needed to schedule an initial appointment with me, urgently. They'd come into my office and tell me their stories. The stories were similar: she was recently divorced, or her husband just died, but either way, he had left her a pile of money (some piles larger than others), and she needed help. These women

- had no idea what their monthly expense needs were;
- were unsure whether this pile of money was going to be enough to take care of them and possibly their children too;
- questioned if they could stay in their houses;
- worried they had to go get a job after being jobless for more than twenty years; and
- asked if they were destined to be bag ladies.

While these concerns are valid if you don't have a financial plan, the disturbing part to me was they all had this one experience in common—they had never been fully responsible for their own money. My heart went out to these women, and I became more convinced than ever that financial education must improve, and it must start at an early age, especially for women.

It doesn't matter whether you came from money or grew up scraping by, you need to understand the basics of managing money—even if your spouse or significant other takes main responsibility for it.

Here are some startling statistics:

- 50 percent of women are nervous about the financial decisions they make, higher among Gen X (58 percent) and Gen Y (57 percent) (2015 Fidelity Investments Money FIT Women Study).
- 3.8 million American women have math skills below a third-grade level (US Department of Education).
- 90 percent of women will be solely responsible for their finances at some point in their lives due to divorce or the death of a spouse (Gender Gap in Financial Literacy 2012).
- 27 percent of married women say they "take control" of financial and retirement planning and manage it themselves. Look at this another way—73 percent of women are not taking control (Prudential 2014 study, Financial Experience and Behaviors among Women).

I've shared with you why I wrote this book, but now let me share with you a little about my personal story. When I was in college in the late 1990s, there was no such thing as a degree in financial planning. There were limited career opportunities in this field. I did not realize it at the time, but I was in a developing and soon-to-be-booming industry at the age of twenty-two. Over the past twenty years, I have had the opportunity to be hired by senior-level executives at Fortune 500 companies to young divorcees who have never had to make a financial decision for themselves. They have trusted me to guide them on their life's journey with their money, advising them on both their personal financial plans and investment strategies.

During my career, I've seen terrifying outcomes due to money: families torn apart squabbling over finances and adult children wasting their lives once they inherited a large amount of assets from their parents. Through my volunteer work in my community supporting homeless families with children, I've seen college-educated women go from stable careers with roofs over their heads and food on the table to being homeless because they lacked basic money skills. Yes, financial disaster can even happen to college-educated women.

The goal of this book is to help you understand the impact money can have on your personal life. It's huge. I want you to have a solid understanding of what it takes to be financially stable and ultimately financially successful. And I never want you to feel you're too paralyzed to make a financial decision—even if you end up on your own unexpectedly. Knowledge is power, especially when it comes to your money.

As we proceed we'll discuss different money experiences you will likely have through your twenties and thirties and how to make wise choices with that money. Keep in mind all of the investment examples I've used are just that – they are examples – and are intended to educate you, not give you specific investment advice. You'll receive some education from this book that you haven't learned in school or heard from your parents. It will help set you up for a comfortable and financially secure life. I realize those are lofty goals, but given my professional experience, I have firsthand experience with how money can ruin or rescue a person.

As you read through this book, keep in mind the advice is coming from both my professional experience and personal experience, and I wish I had learned these lessons at an earlier age. Now, on to you.

CONTENTS

CHAPTER 1

Building Your Reputation and Banking Your Paycheck

Up until about age thirteen, your parents probably provided for 100 percent of your financial needs. As a teenager, you may have entered a period where you earned some money through a babysitting job, lifeguarding at a community pool, or even walking a neighbor's dog. Making your own money is one of the earliest entrees into adulthood, and earning money brings you a level of self-respect and freedom. If you went to college, you may have had to work part-time to help pay for school or just to have pocket money for social activities. If so, you already have a great start to understanding the basics of money, but there's still a lot you need to know.

Here are some money concepts to understand with any job, whether it's part-time or full-time. It could help shape what you want to do with your future career, so let's start with the basics.

What You Get Paid

If your first job was at a grocery store bagging groceries, serving ice cream, lifeguarding, or essentially working for any company, your employer will have determined what they were willing to pay you. In the service industry, this is usually a flat dollar amount for every hour you work. An employer may ask you to commit to a certain number of hours each week or specific days of the week that they need your help.

Many jobs like the above will pay a minimum wage, which is an hourly rate set by the federal government. In 2019, this is $7.25 per hour and has not increased in ten years, which is scary. Some states set a higher minimum wage for workers in that state. For example, California mandates $12.00 per hour in 2019 for employers with more than twenty-six employees. Even though you may start off working in a job that pays only the minimum wage, the longer you work, the better the odds that your employer will give you a raise. The reason employers do this is to incentivize you to work there for a longer period of time. As you gain the skills to do your job well, it's less time your employer needs to train you or make sure you are doing things the right way. Additionally, you may find yourself being the one to show somebody hired after you how to do their job. Reducing the time an employer has to spend finding workers and training them is important because they can spend that time running the business or finding ways to sell more of their products to customers. Paying you more over time or giving you a periodic bonus is a way to encourage you to work hard for them.

If you find yourself working in the same job for twelve months and are not offered a raise, you should think about approaching your boss and asking for one if you feel you have proven yourself worthy. You are not, however, *entitled* to a raise just because time has passed on the calendar. You must earn it. This is a critical life lesson that will carry you throughout your career, especially if you find you are the boss one day.

If You Are Your Own Boss

Your first job may be one where you have to market your services and yourself and dictate what you want to get paid for your services. An example of this could be when you were a teenage babysitter or walking a neighbor's dogs. In these scenarios, one must first determine how to get the word out. You need to market yourself. As a teen, you may have created flyers to post around your community, informing your neighbors about what you were offering. If this is your chosen path as an adult, you must be ready to communicate why someone should hire you, the type of training you have, what you've done to prepare yourself, why you should be trusted, and so on. Getting the word out can be the hardest part of the job. That's true in business in general, and it will become more obvious as you go through adulthood.

Next, you need to be prepared to quote your fee. This requires some up-front research. What do people your age charge for a similar service? Don't be surprised if you need to start off charging less than the competition; in order to get someone's business, they need to be compelled to hire you and feel your fee is reasonable. And you may be stealing away business from someone else. It sounds mean, but it's business and not personal. You'll hear that phrase over and over again in your future.

In business, you'll learn that your reputation is your most precious asset. Being reliable and doing what you say you are going to do, when you are going to do it, goes a long way. If you are hired to work in a nine-to-five job, show up at 8:45 consistently. *Never* be late. And be flexible if a project deadline is looming and your team is behind. Be the first to pitch in, work longer, go the extra mile, and offer to take the lead. This will not only win the respect of your coworkers but your boss as well. Just make sure you're not letting others take advantage of your willingness to roll up your sleeves; what goes around had better come around.

Be aware there is always competition for your job. You can command more pay once you have a reputation as a stellar performer. If there is demand for your services, people will be willing to pay more. But you can't expect top dollar if you don't have a reputation built, and you must be humble enough to start from the ground and work your way up. Your mom or dad may be a senior executive, but that does not mean *you* have earned anything.

When you have a job, others are relying on you for an outcome. You are being given a certain level of responsibility to fulfill a promise. Do not disappoint. Take pride in your work. You will feel great about yourself, and others will treat you well.

What to Do with Your Paycheck

There are three things you can do with the money that you earn. The first is to spend it. In your twenties or right out of college, you will have very few fixed expenses; rent, insurance, and a car payment are the typical ones. However, there are other basic expenses you need to plan for: food, a data plan, utilities, gas, and the like.

Many other expenses are discretionary: going to the movies with friends, buying a new pair of jeans, going out for dinner and drinks, or purchasing a birthday present for a friend or family member. As you get older, your fixed expenses will be where you'll spend most of your money, although throughout life, you'll really just want to spend your money on discretionary expenses. It's more fun! We'll dive into expenses further in the next chapter.

During my career, I've found one of the hardest things for people to do is to save their money. That's the second thing you can do—and need to do—with the money you earn. The habit of saving a certain percentage of your earnings now and keeping this discipline throughout your entire working life is crucial. One of my favorite phrases I heard early on in my professional career was to "pay yourself first." This means you must determine how much you need or want to save from every dollar you earn, set that aside in a savings or investment account (more on this later), and then the rest of your earnings are free to be spent on your fixed and discretionary expenses. I recommend saving a minimum of 10 percent—ideally 20 percent—of every dollar you earn. For example, if you earn a thousand dollars after taxes per week in your first job, plan to save two hundred dollars a week for future needs like a down payment on a house, a cash emergency fund, retirement, and so on. Have a plan for what type of savings or investment account to put that into.

The third thing you can do with the money you earn is to give it away to charity or someone less fortunate. This is your *giving* plan. Some families have a discipline of giving away or tithing 10 percent of their earnings to charity or a church. If this is a value you have too, determine what institutions you want to benefit and either set up a separate bank account for this cash or give it out right away. Don't feel compelled to donate that money every week or every month. Do some research and determine which charitable causes or needy people could really benefit from your hard-earned money. This may be a place of worship, a local animal shelter, or a friend who is less fortunate than you who can't afford to always go to the movies (you can buy her ticket occasionally). Talk to your parents about their giving values and spend time thinking about your attitude toward helping those in need.

Taxes

I have yet to meet the person who likes paying income taxes, but this is a part of life if you make money. When you get hired for any job, you'll be asked to complete an employee withholding allowance certificate (Form W-4), which can be done on paper or electronically. This is where you need to elect how much you want taken out of your paycheck for income taxes. If it's not enough by the end of the year, you'll owe the Internal Revenue Service (IRS) each year when you file your annual income tax return. That can be an awful shock and an unplanned expense for anyone.

In your first job, if you are single, electing "Single, 0 exemptions" on your W-4 will probably be a good move since that's on the higher end of how much tax you are instructing your employer to take out of your paycheck. There are online calculators where you can enter your salary, and they will show you how much your take-home pay will be, after tax withholdings. Most states have an income tax rate, and don't forget you'll be paying federal income tax, state income tax, and FICA and Medicare, which go to the Social Security system in the United States. It can be alarming to see how much lower your take-home pay is compared to your before-tax salary. It is critical you don't overlook this when building your budget.

Banking

With the money you earn, regardless of whether it's for spending, saving, or giving, find a bank you are comfortable with that offers all the conveniences and features you are looking for. Many banks offer online spending analyses, free bill pay, overdraft protection, round-up programs (where a few pennies from each purchase is deducted from your checking and added to your savings—I love that feature) and other perks to make monitoring your money easy. Above all, make sure the bank doesn't slap you with excess fees. If you know you can't commit to keeping a $2,500 minimum balance in your checking account each month, don't select that type of account just because it may pay a little higher interest rate! If you fall below the $2,500 minimum, all of your interest is probably eaten up in the fees you'll be charged—and you'll still likely owe fees on top of that lost interest.

I'll get very basic here for a moment if you're a banking novice. One type of bank account is called a checking account, and these accounts typically have debit cards attached to them. A debit card is a small rectangular piece of plastic with a magnetic strip that you can swipe or insert into a device at a store to purchase something. When you swipe the card at the checkout register, the money you spend is automatically subtracted from your checking account balance. Keep that in mind if you have $500 in your checking account, you can't swipe your debit card for something that costs $520 unless you have overdraft protection and the money comes out of savings. A debit card can also be used in ATMs to withdraw cash from your checking account, and the same rule applies here: if you have $100 in your checking account you can't type in $120 for your withdrawal from the ATM.

While the account is called a checking account, the bank will issue you checks, which are slips of paper that you can use to buy something at a store or pay a bill like your cell phone bill. Checks are used a lot less frequently these days, and you may find you don't need to use them for many years (if ever, depending on the future of banking!) The first time I wrote a check was to pay for part of my first college tuition bill, and it was over $10,000. I remember that experience vividly.

When I was a teenager, I would save almost all of my money and put it into a plastic Solo cup. Every few months, we'd go as a family into the city to deposit it into my bank account. Plus, and I did not know this, my parents had also been putting money into my account from the time I was a baby. This was how we were saving for my college education: together. When my first tuition bill came from the college, my mom had me write the check from my account. The amount on that check was higher than I could have ever imagined paying. It was also my first lesson in how to write out a check, and my mom had to show me how to do it. I was clueless and intimidated.

You can walk into a bank branch and get an application to open a checking account, or you can do so online or through an app (much simpler). You'll need to do some research to decide which bank to open your checking account with. Again, I typically suggest one that is convenient to you. Which bank is closest to where you live or has ATMs in places you go to often?

In addition to the checking account, set up a savings account that will serve as your first place to build savings. More on this soon.

CHAPTER 2

The Sweet-or-Sour Taste of Self-Sufficiency

Budgets, Bank Accounts, and Dealing with Debt

Your first full-time job out of college brings a lot of financial freedom. It can feel like a huge windfall to have all of this money—and you get to decide how to spend it! But do it right, ladies. This time in your life is critical for setting the foundation for your future financial success.

Building a Budget

Building a budget is not hard, but it takes focused time to think through where your money needs to go. There are many online tools you can use to get started and track your spending, such as Mint.com. As discussed in the previous chapter, expenses come in two categories: basic/fixed and discretionary. Some general categories of basic expenses are food, housing (rent), insurance (car, home/renters, health, life, disability), clothing (to an extent!), medications, household supplies (cleaning), utilities (water, gas, electric, garbage, data plan), transportation (car payment—again within reason—gasoline, bus/cab/train fares). Basic expenses are essentially needed to live a standard life and get by day-to-day. Determine what basic expenses need to be covered and make sure you have extra from your paycheck for beyond these basics.

Discretionary expenses are not needed to live day-to-day, and this is often where someone's spending can get out of line. Examples in this category are dining out, vacations, extra clothing above basic needs (which is likely most of what you are buying!), gifts, charitable donations, music/TV subscriptions, and other recreational or social activities. When building a budget, you'll want to aim at keeping your basic/fixed expenses as reasonable as possible so that you have room for fun money (your discretionary spending.) Another reason is that if you find yourself short on cash, you can then cut back on your discretionary spending and not run up credit card debt. It's imperative you learn this life skill. If you don't have the cash to pay your expenses, you need to stop spending money and cut back!

Credit Card Debt

Buying something on credit is using someone else's money to buy something for yourself. Having credit means you have a history of borrowing money and paying it back or paying your bills on time, including electric bills, water bills, and property taxes. Once you start the process of borrowing money or having bills in your name, you'll start having a credit score, which is a number that indicates how trustworthy you are in paying your bills on time or paying back your debts on time. Although there are various companies that have their own measurements of credit, generally a credit score will range between 300 and 850. A score under 600 is concerning to banks or other lending institutions. Banks will often charge a higher rate of interest to people with low credit scores who want to borrow money.

For many young adults, attractive credit card offers, special deals for recent college grads, or even booths set up on college campuses by the major credit companies are like a wolf luring its unsuspecting prey into the dark woods. The 2009 Credit CARD Act prevented college students under the age of twenty-one from opening a credit account themselves, but they still can get one with a parent cosigning. Despite the intention of the act, the critical life lessons about managing credit card debt are often not taught before the shopping spree temptation exposes itself.

In the case of credit cards, there are companies that are lending you money to buy a product or pay for a service, and if you don't pay them back in full within thirty days, they begin to charge interest. And this interest can get very high— easily north of 20 percent. There will be a minimum required payment each month, but don't fall into that trap. It does not mean you should just pay the minimum; this is simply a small amount that is required each month to avoid defaulting on your promise to pay back the credit card company for your purchase. Credit card payback patterns have a major impact on your personal credit score. Paying off your credit cards each month, regularly, for several years can result in an excellent credit score! Having strong credit is a key element in setting yourself up for lifelong financial security.

However, not paying credit card bills is a major reason people destroy their personal credit score, and it can lead to a lifetime of financial pressure—or even financial disaster. Not making minimum monthly payments on credit cards and not having a consistent pattern of paying the card balances in full each month lowers a person's credit score. A wise piece of advice I've heard over the years is that if you don't have the cash in your bank account right now to pay for the purchase, you should not buy it. Discipline is so hard for many people, especially when a quick swipe or tap of a credit card is all you need.

Let's say you buy a new jacket for $100, and your minimum monthly payment is $10. You forget to make your first monthly payment, and the 20 percent interest starts accruing. Now you owe the credit card company $101.67. After a year of not paying for your $100 jacket, the jacket now costs you $121.94 with the interest adding up monthly. And it's probably worse than that because if you kept missing your monthly payments, the credit card company will raise your interest rate—and it may even turn you over to a credit collection agency that can enforce legal action against you. This can spiral out of control.

Whenever you want to make a large purchase like a house or a new car, your credit report will be reviewed by the bank on the lending side. That impacts what rate of interest they offer you, and if there is a pattern of not paying down your credit cards or making your regular payments, you may not get a new loan at all. Spiraling further, not paying off your credit cards can lead you to declare bankruptcy, which ruins your credit score and your ability to borrow any more for seven years. When you apply for a job, many companies will pull your credit score. If they see it's a mess, which shows irresponsibility on your end, you probably won't get the job. If you don't have a job, how will you pay cash for your expenses? You certainly can't pay on credit anymore! You can see how bad credit can impact your entire life.

Student Loans

While there are books and other resources that totally focus on this topic, I want to highlight that student loans can become a huge fixed expense for someone after they graduate college—and for many years thereafter. I have a neighbor who went to elite graduate school programs, and after factoring in tuition and living expenses, she built up over $200,000 of student loan debt before the age of thirty.

A mountain of debt can feel insurmountable and overwhelming. It must become part of your basic/fixed budget and will impact how nice of an apartment you can afford, the type of car you can afford to drive, how often you can go partying with your friends, and how frequently you can go on vacation. Debt impacts your quality of life. When you can control your debt, you can control your quality of life. Pay off your student loans as fast as you can.

The Emergency Fund

This is a lifelong critical component to your financial well-being. An emergency fund is having cash in a savings account that can be tapped into when you, periodically, have to exceed your planned monthly budget. For example, you probably didn't factor into your budget the new set of tires on your used car you suddenly need to get after running over a set of nails, the new laptop purchase after your old one crashed, or the unexpected plane ticket home to see a sick relative. However, these are "life happens" type expenses, and you need to be prepared for them once in a while. If you are not prepared, you're going to rack up credit card debt, and over time, that can spiral out of control.

It's a good rule of thumb to build an emergency fund, a rainy day fund, of three to six months of your living expenses. For example, if your month-to-month expenses average $3,000, then you should target building a separate savings account between $9,000 and $18,000. As your living expenses increase over time, so should the extra cash you have set aside in your emergency fund. When you do have to tap into this, be sure to build it back up as soon as you can.

The first few years of your working adult life, you may find this is the one and only savings strategy you can afford to do, but it's truly the foundation for which to build the rest of your financial plan. Another reason this is so critical is to protect you from being stuck in a miserable job. You always want to give yourself the financial flexibility to quit and walk right out the door if your job becomes overbearing, you don't agree with the business practices, or you feel you're being treated unfairly. Even if you get a great job offer that's clear across the country, you're going to need some extra cash to physically make this move or pay back any sign-on bonuses you may forfeit with your current company.

I cannot stress enough the importance of always having this emergency fund intact. As time goes on, if you get married and have children, it may be worthwhile to have a six-to-twelve-month emergency fund in place, especially if only one spouse or partner works. When there are more expenses and more people relying on you financially, that calls for a bigger bank balance set aside.

CHAPTER 3

Buying a Car and Protecting Your Rear End

In your teenage years, one of the biggest thrills you may have experienced was having your own set of wheels. It brought freedom. Mom or Dad were no longer shuttling you around to your friends' houses, social activities, or Friday night high school football games. Driving yourself around made you feel more mature and more grown-up.

Cars, even for adults, can also be a status symbol. The fancier the car you drive, the more the perception will be that you have more money than other people. It also means you'll have to spend a lot of money to keep up with the latest and greatest in auto trends! Did you know that new cars lose value the second you drive them off the car lot? As soon as you pay all that money for a car, it's worth less as soon as you take ownership. Cars and trucks are depreciating assets, meaning they are worth less the longer you own them. They are machines; the parts wear down over time and eventually need to get replaced since machines don't work forever.

Your parents may have purchased your first vehicle for you, and if that was the case, consider yourself very lucky! But in having this luck, your parents prevented you from having a major life experience that will teach you about money. Even if you are now the one paying for your first (or next) car, through money you've earned and money you've saved, you need to understand what the experience of buying or having your first major asset could bring about.

Buying Your First Car—New or Used?

There are many places you can buy a car or truck. One option is a private sale—one between you and someone else who owns the vehicle. In this transaction, the seller will offer their vehicle for sale at a certain price, and it's common you will negotiate with them on the final sales price. The seller may not budge off their initial offer, but it's always worth asking for a lower price. Remember, the car or truck will be worth less every day that you drive it. The seller will either want you to pay them in cash or provide you with a cashier's check, which is a check from your bank, paid to the seller. The bank deducts the cash from your bank account when they provide you with the check to give to the seller. That gives the seller assurance the check won't bounce, meaning there is enough money in your bank account to pay for the vehicle. If the seller accepts a personal check from you, they run the risk that you don't actually have enough cash in your bank account—and you've left with their vehicle! Online payment services like Venmo, PayPal, and others make transferring money to others very easy and convenient without the above risks, and these are constantly evolving. Yet big purchases may be beyond the limits of these online payment services, and in many cases, fees do apply.

When you purchase the vehicle, the seller needs to give you the title to the car, a piece of paperwork that proves you legally own the vehicle. You may take out a private loan from a bank to buy this vehicle, and since the bank will charge you interest each day you owe them money, pay this loan off ASAP.

Another option for purchasing a vehicle is to go to a business that sells used cars. These are called used car lots or used car dealerships. Sometimes these dealerships will arrange financing for you, meaning you can take out a loan there to buy the vehicle. You'll typically find a wide variety of vehicles to choose from, and the used car dealership has likely purchased these vehicles from an assortment of places (auctions, individuals, other dealerships, etc.) Keep in mind they are looking to make a profit no matter how good a deal they say you are receiving.

One of the concerns with buying a used car is you're never 100 percent certain what the history of that car is. Prior accidents should be reported and available to you, but the way the prior owner(s) treated the vehicles or the road conditions it was driven in are not always known. There is some risk in buying a used car, and you'll hope you don't end up facing major expensive repairs shortly after you buy it. Some dealerships will offer a limited warranty on the vehicle to give peace of mind in the quality of vehicle you are buying, and if anything major goes wrong during the warranty period, the cost will likely be covered so you don't have to pay for the repairs yourself.

Finally, you can buy a vehicle from a new car dealership (they often also have used cars there for sale too). You can get financing to purchase the vehicle through the dealership, and again, they are looking to make a profit too. New cars come with warranties that are often more thorough and longer than those for used cars. Other perks may be added to your purchase, including free oil changes if you come back to the dealership to get that maintenance work done, since the dealership wants you to visit often to keep you as a customer.

Getting a Loan

At your age, it may be hard to qualify for a loan yourself. Your parents may need to be a cosigner, which means they are liable for paying back your loan if you can't. One of the reasons you may not qualify without someone else cosigning is that you may not have had a steady job for a long enough period of time to show the bank you have regular income (a main criteria for banks to know whether you can afford to pay them back) or have built enough credit.

Let's say you want to borrow $10,000 and have an excellent credit score with a stable paycheck. The bank will want to loan you money because you'll be seen as a good, reliable customer with a high probability of paying back your loan. Let's say the bank offers you their best car loan rate of 5 percent. If your credit score is low or damaged—or you don't have a stable paycheck—the bank is taking a bigger risk in lending you money. The bank, if they decide to offer you a loan, could charge you 7 percent, 10 percent, or more. Buying that same car could cost you significantly more if your credit score is low! People in this scenario are usually better off delaying their car purchase, trying to save as much money as they can, and paying cash for the car (or borrowing as little as possible). Asking Mom or Dad to cosign can be embarrassing as a young adult. It's key to always pay your bills and pay your debts on time.

The Car-Buying Experience—Ladies Beware!

I remember the first time I went to buy a car. I had just graduated college, and my parents were kind enough to give me their used Pontiac Sunbird (a sporty looking two-door aqua blue car) while I was in college. They said I could either keep the car or use it for a trade-in toward the purchase of a newer car. Well, knowing I had secured a nice full-time job in upstate New York, paying a solid $28,000 per year (in 1999), I figured I must, just must, have some fancy wheels to take me to my fancy finance job!

My dad and I scoured the dealerships looking for just the right car for me. And I found it: a bright, shiny red, brand-new Pontiac Grand Am spinning slowly on a rotating wheel in the middle of the new car dealership's showroom floor. It was on display for all to see, and it just had to be mine. The price tag was around $20,000—almost what I was to earn in an entire year!

My dad and I sat down with the salesman and started to negotiate. Really, my dad did all the talking, and I just sat back and watched it all happen. I remember being slightly uncomfortable during the negotiating process. I really wanted the car, but I was exhausted and frustrated sitting at the salesman's desk. He kept having to go back to his manager with our latest offer. Finally, after several hours of back-and-forth, we agreed on a price.

We got my financing through the dealership, and the monthly payment seemed reasonable. At the time, I had not moved into my first apartment, so I really had no idea what my car budget should be. I just knew that I got to drive home a really shiny, fancy red car! Real world, look out—here I come! Am I the smartest, coolest, most savvy young woman or what?

Fast-forward less than a year later, and I had been relocated to Atlanta with my finance job. My car was shipped down from New York and unloaded in the parking lot of the apartment complex where I was renting. When I moved to Atlanta, I did not know anybody. At the age of twenty-two, I felt total excitement and confidence, and being alone and independent did not concern me one bit.

Then my fancy red car started to have mechanical issues. I found a dealership and took it in for repairs. And I had to bum rides off of my coworkers, which was awkward since I really did not know them well enough to keep asking for favors. In those days, Uber and Lyft did not exist. Taxis, in the suburban area I was living, were not readily available. The real-life lesson of the importance of reliable transportation hit me like a rock. I quickly realized, after several trips to the car repair shop and continuing issues, I needed a reliable vehicle. How would I find that? Well, once again, I looked to my parents for guidance and decided to buy the same car my mom had: an Infiniti G4. A nice, four-door, standard-looking sedan with a leather interior.

Well, my dad was nine hundred miles away, so I knew I'd be on my own trying to buy this car. I found an Infiniti dealership, went in one day, and started to negotiate on a new silver Infiniti that had just arrived on the lot (and it was not on the showroom floor!) I asked questions about the warranty, checked out the gas mileage, evaluated which options I needed versus those I wanted (like the sunroof: a want but not a need), and sat down at the salesman's desk.

When he came back with his first offer and told me what the monthly payments would be, much to his surprise, I pulled out my financial calculator and ran a quick calculation on what the implied interest rate on that loan was. Punching in the monthly payment, the term of the loan (four years), and the sale price of the car, I hit the "solve for" button. It came back showing a 20 percent interest rate! *What? Is this guy serious?* He must have figured I was a young, naïve, single female who could be taken advantage of, but what he did not know was that I was a finance major in college, had a job in finance, and could call his bluff.

I rebuked, we negotiated further, and we settled on a much more reasonable sale price and loan structure. I walked out of there a few hours later, with my financial calculator in hand, as the proud owner of a much more reserved, but reliable, car. I kept that car for eight years and never had a problem with it. The only reason I sold it was that I was pregnant with twins and needed more room in the back for two large car seats. I sold it for cash to a friend who was buying his daughter a reliable car for college. He knew me, and he knew I took care of my belongings. His daughter has graduated college with my Infiniti still running smoothly.

Even though I'm a partner in a successful wealth-management firm in Atlanta, I still dread the thought of buying my next car. As the process of buying a car is done more in the e-commerce world today, this provides a shield against the sometimes-unscrupulous car salesperson and the negative experience often associated with buying a car. Much research and price negotiating can be done online, saving time and headaches, and I highly recommend going this route initially to avoid hassles.

Car Insurance

When you own a car, you need car insurance. And the younger you are, the more it costs! A large part of the equation of how much car you can afford is how much the insurance on that car (and the driver) will cost. Insurance companies know that young drivers have less experience handling the roadways than those who have been driving for decades, and they price the insurance accordingly. When you are under the age of twenty-five, car insurance can cost several hundred dollars a month.

Basic car insurance coverage is comprehensive coverage and collision coverage. Many people choose to not carry collision insurance if their car is not worth much money, meaning it would not be a financial hardship if your car was totaled and you had to buy a new one. Car insurance covers the cost of repairs for you and/or the other car(s) if you are in an accident or if your car is stolen or damaged by a major storm, fire, or vandalism. It also covers medical bills if you or someone else experiences an injury from a car accident. There are extras you can add to the insurance plan, such as towing cost reimbursement and rental car cost reimbursement (if your car needs major repairs after an accident, and you need to rent a car). Some states require drivers to have uninsured motorist coverage, which protects you in the event someone causes damage to your car (or you/your passengers) but does not carry their own car insurance.

When you become an adult, shopping around for car insurance companies and rates that may be more competitive than your current policy is wise to do every three years. One hint that's personally worked for me is to ask the insurance agent, "Are there any new discounts that I qualify for?" Whenever you are buying car insurance, be sure to know what programs or discounts may be available to you, especially as a young person when your rates are high.

Protecting Your Rear End

Inside every automobile insurance policy is a limit of liability protection that comes into play if you are sued and found responsible for an accident or mistake that causes harm to someone else. When you are young, you'll likely look for the lowest available limits of liability coverage that the insurance company will offer you since you have very few assets at risk if you get sued. However, if you are not properly insured for liability, your entire financial situation could be at risk, including future paychecks.

An umbrella policy or excess liability policy is extra insurance you should buy in addition to the liability limits in your auto policy. For example, the umbrella policies come in increments of $1 million, and a good rule of thumb is to have one times your net worth (assets minus debts) in liability coverage. You should buy more if your risks are higher. When you have a full-time job, even if you are not worth $1 million, consider buying one of these umbrella policies, which you can get through your home/auto insurance agent. They are relatively inexpensive for the amount of coverage they provide.

CHAPTER 4

Starting Off on the Right Financial Foot—Your First Big-Time Job

It may take a few years of less-than-desirable jobs for you to finally secure your first big-time job. This is a job you want given your skills and interests, that pays a healthy salary, and provides upward mobility. If you are lucky, perhaps this actually is your first job out of college. Perhaps it comes your way after graduate school. Regardless, this is a pivotal point in starting retirement savings and having discretionary income to begin building wealth, getting out of debt, particularly student loans, and saving for the largest purchase of your life: a house.

Maximizing the Compensation and Benefit Plans at Work

If you received the promotion you were seeking or landed that next big job, this is a huge personal accomplishment and financial opportunity. First and foremost, do not start spending your big paycheck before you receive it. Better yet, have a plan for this extra money before your first big paycheck is cut!

If you are working in the private sector, you will typically have access to a retirement plan like a 401(k) savings plan. In the public sector, the similar type plan is called a 403(b) plan. This is an investment account where you can elect to have a certain amount of your paycheck directly deposited into the investment account, which is a way to save for your retirement. Many employers will match a portion of what you save into your account. But don't be fooled! Maxing out your 401(k) plan does not mean putting in the minimum amount just to get the maximum "free" employer matching dollars. The government sets a limit each year as to how much money someone can defer into their 401(k) or 403(b) savings account. In 2019, that amount is $19,000 if you are under age fifty. To truly be maxing out your retirement savings account, you should target the $19,000 government limit and not just the 3 percent or 5 percent that your employer may match. This is one of the biggest financial mistakes I see people make.

For example, let's say you are now earning $100,000, and your employer will match 50 percent of the first 6 percent you contribute. You decide to contribute 6 percent, in order to get the free employer matching deposit of 3 percent (50 percent of 6 percent = 3 percent). Your employer will put in $3,000 if you put in $6,000. But, in order to truly max out, which should be the ultimate goal of every professional, you need to contribute 19 percent of your pay to your 401(k) / 403(b) savings plan.

Here is an example of the benefits of compounded growth. If you are thirty years old and land your big job, making $100,000 per year, and decide to save 6 percent of your pay into your 401(k) plan, after twenty years that can accumulate to $198,000 at age fifty (using a sample 5 percent annual investment return). If you really push yourself and set a target of saving the government maximum limit set of $19,000, at age fifty, you'll have more than triple: $628,000! Every dollar saved today can turn into multiple dollars for you in the future.

Many retirement plans give you the option of saving before-tax dollars (also called pre-tax) into your retirement plan or saving after-tax dollars into a Roth 401(k) plan. If you elect to save on a pre-tax basis, the amount you save goes into the 401(k) before taxes are assessed on your paycheck, which lowers the amount you pay in tax today. However, when you take money out of your account in retirement, you'll pay income taxes on all the money you withdraw from the investment account. (While the money is growing inside the 401(k) / 403(b) plan, you are not paying taxes on the growth). With a Roth 401(k), the amount you save into it does not reduce your taxes today, but you won't pay income taxes in retirement on the money you take out (given today's tax laws). Generally, the lower the federal and state income tax brackets you fall into now, the more enticing putting money into the Roth 401(k) is.

One of the best pieces of financial advice I ever received, and I have followed it religiously, is to increase the amount you are saving into your 401(k) plan every time you get a raise.

If you don't have the extra cash in your bank account, you're not going to get used to spending it! For example, if you get a 3 percent raise, instead of saving say 6 percent into your 401(k), increase it to 9 percent. You'll quickly be able to afford maxing out your 401(k) or 403(b) plan by following this piece of advice without having to make financial sacrifices.

Investing Your Retirement Account

The younger you are, generally the more stocks you should own in your retirement account. The reason is that stocks have historically grown in value more than cash, bonds, and other investments. Owning a stock is owning a small piece of a company (such as Coca-Cola, Home Depot, Google, or Facebook). Owning a bond is lending money to a company or a government agency for a specific period of time with the promise they'll pay you back your money at a future date (the bond's maturity). While you own the bond, the company or government agency pays you a predefined rate of interest. The closer you get to retirement, the more bonds you should own in your retirement accounts since they will be more stable in value and generate income for you to live on. Stocks can go up and down a lot more than bonds, but over time, stocks tend to generate average investment returns of around 7 percent annualized (based on historical data going back to 1950). Bonds tend to have an average return that is half of stocks. A very important point you need to understand about stock and bond performance is that it's never guaranteed! Just because stocks have historically outperformed bonds doesn't mean that will always be the case in the future. We just have history to look back on and see what the trends have been.

Many retirement plans offer you a preset mix of investment funds to choose from. Some have online tools you can use to determine what percentage you should have in stocks, bonds, or real estate investments. Using these tools will give you reasonable guidance if you don't have a professional to advise you. Having 100 percent in stocks at age thirty may feel unsettling, especially when you see your value temporarily go down, but you've got twenty or thirty years before you'll need to touch your retirement money. And there is a risk of your money not growing for you over this time. If your investments don't grow enough for you, you'll need to work longer, cut back later in life, and save more or spend less. Your health later on in life may not allow you to work full-time. At a minimum, someone in their twenties or thirties should have at least 80 percent in stocks or stock-like investments.

Who else can give you advice? Don't just look to your parents; they may or may not be familiar with the types of financial opportunities and decisions in front of you. Many people's parents have pensions, which are pretty much like dinosaurs these days! Consider asking a colleague at work who seems to have it all together, ask your boss or another mentor for guidance, or consult with a fee-only or hourly financial advisor.

Consider the *target retirement date* or *asset allocation funds* most 401(k) and 403(b) plans offer, which are a preset mix of stocks and bonds and US and international investments, and a team of investment professionals at that mutual fund company is deciding how to shift the investment mix each year. It's like putting your investment strategy on autopilot, and the investment mix becomes more conservative the closer you get to retirement age. I tend to say you don't need to hire a professional to give you guidance and invest your money until you have at least $250,000. But if you do, you can find a fee-only (non-commission sales person) in your area on NAPFA.org.

Your Annual Bonus

If you are fortunate enough to receive an annual bonus, be sure you have a plan for that money! The same goes with any extra cash flow you have each month. If you don't have a plan, you are going to spend the extra money and waste a financial opportunity. This savings method will form the basis for your future financial stability.

One example of a plan is to target saving 25 percent of your bonus, use 25 percent to pay down debt, plan for 30 percent going toward taxes on the bonus, and spending 20 percent on yourself. You deserve some enjoyment for all of your hard work too! A big trap I've seen people fall into over the years is getting too comfortable with knowing an annual bonus is coming, and they overspend during the year, using their bonus to bail them out of their credit card debt. If your company has one bad year, and you end up with a one-year membership to the jelly of the month club in lieu of cash, poof! There goes your financial plan.

You can't control whether you'll get a bonus, so don't spend it before it arrives.

I've also seen many families use their annual bonus to pay for their children's private K-12 school expenses, and as much as I value education, I will tell you that parents will not put their children back into public school if they don't get a big bonus one year. These K-12 expenses become part of the family's fixed expense budget items each year, and the bigger your fixed expenses, the less financial flexibility you have.

Protect Your Emergency Fund—and Then Invest

We previously discussed the importance of building an emergency fund equal to three to six months of your living expenses. It's possible that you may find yourself out of a job at some point in your career, and if you have enough money in the bank to pay your bills for a few months, that can protect your credit score, avoid having to tap into retirement savings early (and then incurring a tax penalty), and overall allowing yourself to sleep better with less stress. It can also give you more clarity around what job to accept next. If you are desperate for cash, you'll take any job that comes your way—even if it makes you miserable. With your savings from your new raise or annual bonus, be sure to build up your emergency fund. Make sure this is solid before you start investing in stocks or bonds with your bonus money.

Next, if you are not maximum funding your 401(k) plan with your monthly salary, you can adjust the amount you put into your 401(k) at bonus time, which can help propel you toward your annual savings goals. But you need to make that adjustment before your bonus pays! You can also put money into an IRA or Roth IRA each year. In 2019, the annual amount you can deposit into an IRA or Roth IRA is $6,000 if you are under age fifty. Anyone who has a paycheck can put money into an IRA, but only those who make under certain income limits can put money into a Roth IRA. Putting money into either type of IRA likely won't save you any income taxes to fund these accounts (for the IRA, it depends on your tax situation; Roth IRA contributions are not tax-deductible). However, the money will grow tax-deferred inside the investment account, and in the case of a Roth IRA, it can be withdrawn tax-free in retirement.

Next, you can open a regular brokerage account and invest in a seemingly unlimited number of investments, with no tax penalties or other restrictions as to when you take the money out. You'll pay income taxes each year on the earnings in this investment account (like interest and dividends) and will pay income taxes when you sell an investment inside this account for a profit (a capital gain). However, you will pay less in taxes down the road when you pull out the money, for example, in retirement.

A brokerage account is a good savings tool, especially if you want to retire before age fifty-nine and a half since tax penalties exist on withdrawals from 401(k) or IRA accounts up to that point. Money in this account can also be used to buy your first home, pay for your children's college expenses, or for any other reason you may need to dip into savings while you are working.

Paying Off Debt

My philosophy is that paying down debt should be one component of your annual savings strategy rather than being the entire focus of your financial strategy. I know a lot of people who are debt averse and want to get out of debt as soon as possible. While this is noble, if you are doing so without building an emergency fund, you can find yourself right back in debt. And if you are paying off your mortgage or student loans rapidly, you are not saving enough into something that's liquid where you can tap into it easily should an unexpected life set back occur, or you simply need some extra cash. You can't buy groceries off the equity in your house in retirement—or pay for your kids' college with the equity in your house—unless you take out a new loan, open a line of credit, or use some other form of borrowing against your assets.

While conventional wisdom says to pay off high-interest rate debt first, I like to start with paying off small balances first. You'll experience a sense of achievement and personal satisfaction that will motivate you to keep going. And when that small debt is paid in full, cut up the credit card, hide it, or close out that loan!

Every little bit of debt you can pay down each month will help in the long run, but don't sacrifice your liquidity to get out of debt.

Insurance

The older you are, the more assets you'll have, and when other people start relying on your income, insurance planning becomes even more important. It's wise to always have health insurance. Even when you are single, have a small amount of life insurance—at least enough to pay off any debts you may have like student loans. Disability insurance is very important as this protects your income in case you are injured or suffer a long-term illness, and are unable to work. It won't cover all of your paycheck, but if you think about your biggest asset early in your career, it's your ability to work and earn a paycheck! When you don't have enough savings to pay your expenses for the next twenty or thirty years, insurance is critically important.

Most people get their main insurance coverages through their employers. One consideration is buying a small term life insurance policy and small supplemental disability insurance policy through an individual insurance company, outside of your employer. The premiums can be fixed so the cost won't increase while you own the insurance policy, and you can take the policy with you regardless of where you work or how great (or not so great) your employer's benefits are. Plus, you are better off getting insurance in place while you are young since you may not qualify later in life if you experience a major health setback. Be sure to check out the financial rating of the insurance company you are buying from, which can be found on most insurance company websites (A rated is best). Also, just as in seeking financial advice, get a referral to an insurance agent from someone you trust. The agent can shop the marketplace for you to find the best policy at the best price. Most insurance agents work on commission and are paid by the insurance company, so it does not cost you anything out of pocket to work through an agent.

Career Tips for Your Next Promotion

Assertive women tend to have a negative stereotype in the business world. There are many books about how to manage the male-female dynamic in the workplace. I suggest Gail Evans's *Play Like a Man, Win Like a Woman*, which I read early in my career. One issue you may face is being paid less money than a man who does the same job, and it's not because your company is discriminating against you. It's because men are typically not afraid to ask, boast of their accomplishments, and vocalize their worth. Women tend to be less vocal about their accomplishments and reasons for deserving a raise or promotion. Don't be afraid to speak up and let your manager tactfully know when you've accomplished a big task, done something to make them look good, or added to the company's profitability. This is an art—not a science. If you don't speak up for yourself and take control of your career, nobody else will—and you won't make the extra money you deserve to get paid in the long run.

Another strategy to get a raise, a promotion, or be more successful in the professional world is to find a mentor inside your organization. Look for someone you admire, you feel you can confide in, and takes an interest in you personally and your career. This takes time but keep your eyes open for someone older than you who seems to want to help you. The reason this is important is they've paved a path before you, so they know how to navigate the office politics. They've had their own struggles, found ways to overcome them, and have probably battled what you are about to experience next: the struggle to maintain work-life balance.

CHAPTER 5

Previewing a Painful Choice—Choosing a Career to Match the Balance of Life

While you are young and single, time is not viewed as a precious commodity. You can work the number of hours, including weekends and nights, that you want to and still find time to exercise, socialize, and enjoy the dating scene. Without realizing the time crunch that often comes between ages twenty-eight and thirty-five, you may not be aware that your level of personal freedom is about to get pinched.

You may be pondering certain concepts at this point in your career: "Will this job allow me to have a family one day—without major demands on my time?" "Am I making enough money to warrant giving up time with my family, with my children, when that point in my life comes?" "Can I afford to buy a home I can grow into with a family, if that's in my future?" If the answer to any of these questions is no, you may start reevaluating your career choice. For example, if you are a doctor in the emergency room, you may be working long, grueling hours, including nights, and you sleep during the day. That schedule will be very challenging with young children, but it can be done! On the plus side, you may only need to work a certain number of shifts each month to make a good income, so you could have more time at home than other jobs that require a nine-to-five schedule. If you are a teacher, you have a pretty good work schedule, especially with your summers off, but day care expenses will eat away at a major part of your paycheck.

Decisions about your career path at this point in your life can pave the way to giving up your career, or not, when you start a family. As we'll discuss later in this book, jumping out of the workforce, if you so choose, for a few years will have lifelong financial ramifications. According to a PBS News report in 2016, "A twenty-six-year-old woman who's making $50,000 when she takes three years off of work to attend to a child would leave not just $150,000 in lost wages on the table, but an additional $200,000 in lost wage growth—the cumulative effect of time off on future earnings—and some $165,000 in lost retirement assets and benefits." Leaving the workforce, even for a short period of time, is a major personal and financial decision.

The concept of balance of life is one of the biggest struggles for working women who are also mothers. Many successful women will consider themselves workaholics, but that can quickly change when you become a mother. While you'll be working all the time (at a job and/or at home), being a mother will bring you a different level of satisfaction—and it will help put your life in perspective. No longer will missing a deadline at work seem like the end of the world. You'll learn how to negotiate deadlines better and how to rely more on your coworkers. You will, in general, get better at asking for and accepting help.

You may also place a different emphasis on money. Yes, working full-time will bring more financial security, but it will require some level of sacrifice of your family time. You might not even be married or dating someone significant at this point in your life, but it's not too early to start asking yourself some key questions about your chosen career:

- Am I working in a profession that gives me flexibility to adjust my hours? Can I work remotely? Is travel required? Will I need advanced degrees or credentials in order to move up in my field—and should I get those out of the way now?

- Who is in the role I want now? Is there a female in my company working in the same or similar role I eventually want? Watch her carefully. What level of stress does she have? Is she vocalizing struggles with childcare needs or finding time for herself, given work demands? Is she living a personal and professional life that you admire?

Asking yourself these questions—and watching and observing—could lead you to the conclusion that you need to jump out of this job or your current career path. According to a 2015 study of 1,500 MBA students and graduates published in the

Boston Globe, "Both genders saw the trade-off between career advancement and other life priorities as the biggest obstacle to reaching their professional goals."

One of the best things you can do at this point in your career is have awareness of what may lie ahead for you in your chosen career, determine what you need to accomplish today (more education, more time with the boss, learning new skills, networking), and make sure you're in the right job, the right career path, and alleviating career pressure once you become a mother.

At age twenty-four, I received my MBA by attending a part-time (and highly ranked) program at Georgia State University. Shortly thereafter, I earned my CERTIFIED FINANCIAL PLANNER™ designation. Then at age thirty-two when I was pregnant with our first children, twins, I needed to complete an educational program and pass the test for an investment designation called the CIMA®. This was something my company was requiring in order to advance to the next level. The last phase of this designation required completing a weeklong program at either Wharton in Pennsylvania or Berkeley in California, both top-notch schools. I had always wanted to receive a degree from Wharton—the most prestigious business school in my opinion—but their summer class was already full. And then my doctor told me I couldn't travel after September. The only option was to fly to California for a week and attend the Berkeley session in August. I was barely able to reach over my bulging stomach to write and take notes, and I had to snack constantly during the classes to feed the two babies I was growing. Also, I was the only female in the class.

In the evenings, all of my classmates, many from the large brokerage firms, would stay out late partying. I cuddled up in my pajamas in my hotel room and studied. On the day of the test, the guys around me were totally stressing out (I wasn't surprised!) They lacked confidence because they had not prepared, and quite frankly, they had showed a level of immaturity in how they approached achieving this designation. I was the first one to complete the exam, and as I walked out, many of my classmates looked up at me either in panic or bewilderment. I heard that half of my class failed (I passed), but I had one chance to check this task off my list since there was no way I was going to have time to study once my babies arrived.

I also promised myself that this was it for my formal education. Completing my education before having children was one of the best moves I ever made.

The bottom line is that *now* is the time to take control over your career path, especially if you think you want to continue working once you have a family. One strong piece of advice is that you won't really know the answer until you become a mother. You'll be surprised how much of a tug and pull you'll feel on your heart to spend every waking moment with your baby.

CHAPTER 6

Job Hopping and Taking Your Money with You

It's normal to land a job out of college, get a few years of experience under your belt, and jump to another opportunity at a different company that better meets your career, financial, and/or lifestyle goals. Yet one of the big financial mistakes young people make is either leaving too much money on the table when they depart their prior employer or not taking what they've built in retirement savings with them.

Before You Leave, Decide Why You Are Leaving

Before you get too excited about the offer letter you just received, and perhaps the big raise you think you're getting by moving on, understand that sometimes the grass is not greener on the other side. More money and greater benefits are not appealing paired with a toxic environment where you and your coworkers are miserable.

Why are you leaving your current job? Is it only because of money? Do you dislike your boss or the projects you are working on? Is there no opportunity for advancement? Before starting to look on the outside, if you have found an internal mentor, talk with them. They can give you advice on whether the grass is greener somewhere else (they've likely worked at other places), and they can advise you how to make your situation at this job better. Talk with your manager and let them know what concerns you have. You may be surprised how valued you are there, but nobody took the time to tell you! If they think you are a flight risk, and they don't want to lose you, your current employer may increase your compensation to entice you to stay.

I made the mistake early on in my career of not vocalizing my concerns at work, and I looked outside for my next opportunity. I did this twice, in my first and second job. In hindsight, I would have learned a lot more and advanced my skills more quickly had I stayed in Job #1. However, I was fearful of where my career path was headed (very poor work-life balance and extensive travel) even though that next big opportunity would not have presented itself to me for five years. In my second job, I was working my tail off, but I was not receiving many accolades, and I was not sure if I had what it took to be a success there.

I ventured on to Job #3, which was a total disaster. It was 100 percent commission, and after six months, I had made $0. Really. The day I told Job #2 I was resigning, they pleaded with me to stay and offered me a great opportunity working directly with the top financial advisor in that organization—and they told me they were planning to offer me this anyway. Had I just spoken up about my concerns, I probably would still be there today and still had a successful career. I do believe you can make a path to success in more than one place!

Before You Leave, Know What You Are Leaving Behind

There are financial ramifications to leaving your job. First, understand your 401(k) employer match vesting schedule. Are you vested in the money your employer has put into your 401(k)? If you leave within, for example, three years of your hire date, you'll forfeit some or all of the employer match. (The money you put in yourself is always 100 percent vested—you'll never forfeit that.) If your employer offers a pension plan, the same concept applies to that benefit too. There is a vesting schedule. Any company money forfeited will set you behind for your retirement goals. You'll need to find out how soon you can enroll in your new company's 401(k) plan. Is there a waiting period? What you contributed to your former employer's 401(k) plan this year counts against how much you can put into your new company's 401(k) plan later in the same year, in terms of not exceeding the IRS annual limit of $19,000 (in 2019).

Next, if you have a job that pays a bonus, understand the last day you need to be employed in order to receive that bonus. For example, if your bonus pays on March 1 of each year, do you need to be on the payroll December 31 of the prior year? If so, don't quit your job on December 30!

Insurance planning is very important. Will you have a gap in health insurance coverage? Will you need to go on COBRA? (That's expensive, temporary health insurance.) Be sure you get your medications refilled before you start your new job and look into a temporary major medical-only policy to bridge any gap if you don't have ongoing chronic conditions that need regular medical treatment. There could be a waiting period before you start any new health insurance, and your deductibles will start over.

Life insurance may be portable—meaning you may be able to convert your former group life insurance policy to a permanent one—but this typically will be very expensive. The reason is that the only people who take their group life insurance with them are those who are unhealthy and can't qualify for cheaper life insurance with an outside company. This is one reason to have your own term life insurance policy that is not tied to your job!

Disability insurance is typically not portable, meaning you can't take it with you from one job to the next. This is another reason to have your own disability insurance policy outside of your company plan.

Tuition reimbursement

Did your company pay for some or all of your graduate school or even your undergraduate degree? Did you sign a contract saying you would pay this back if you leave within a certain amount of time? I had this happen to me. My first employer paid for most of my MBA tuition, and I needed to stay at least twelve months after the final reimbursement was made—or else I needed to pay back a pro rata amount. That was the one and only time I had to go back to my parents and ask them for money—$1,600—once I started working. I still feel guilty about that.

Finally, if you are high enough in an organization where you receive stock awards, consider the vesting schedule for those as well. This could be money left on the table unnecessarily, but many professionals are able to negotiate forfeited stock awards as a sign-on bonus with their new employer (again if you are high enough in an organization.)

Moving Out Your Money

According to a recent study by benefits consulting firm Aon Hewitt, "More than half of workers in their twenties who leave a job do not roll their 401(k) into an IRA or their new employer's plan." When you leave your job, you can roll over your 401(k) to an IRA or Roth IRA, or to your new job. It's best to move the money somewhere and not leave it at your old job. It will be too easily forgotten—and harder to track and manage. You won't be made aware as soon as regular employees when the investment lineup changes, and you could be assessed higher fees. I personally ran into this situation several years ago with my husband, an engineer. He is really smart with science- and math-related items, but finance was not his strong suit. He did not take action on his 401(k) plans when he left his jobs, and it took a while to wrestle the accounts down. One was sitting mainly in cash (ugh), but we eventually got them rolled into one IRA where our other investment accounts were located. That cut down the number of user names and passwords we need to remember, and it reduced the time it takes to manage this money since it's all in one place!

Which Is Best?

Should you move your new 401(k) to an IRA? What I look at as a financial advisor is whether the new 401(k) has good investments to choose from and what the fees are. Small companies typically have higher fees in their retirement plans and fewer investment choices. IRAs have unlimited investment choices, and you can buy many low-cost or no-cost investments inside of IRAs. And once you roll your old 401(k) plan into your new 401(k) plan, you may not be able to get that money out of there until you leave the new job. Money in an IRA can be moved to almost any financial institution that offers IRAs—whenever you want.

Regardless of where you move your old 401(k) plan, be sure to do a *direct rollover,* which is where the money is moved directly to the new institution. Another option is to have a check payable to your new 401(k) plan or IRA and handing the check to that institution. It's never a good idea to cash out your 401(k) plan and deposit the check into your bank account because you'll pay federal and state income taxes on that money—plus penalties.

If you took out a loan from your 401(k) plan, it likely needs to be paid back ASAP once you leave your company. Otherwise, it turns into a tax nightmare for you. It's rarely a good idea to take a loan from your 401(k) plan. You can't take a loan out of an IRA, and I don't want to talk about this bad idea further!

If you have stock in your former company, you can move those shares to a brokerage account, which is best for ease of managing and tracking. Some employers will start charging annual account fees to former employees who leave their stocks in the former employer's sponsored brokerage account.

Negotiating Your New Job Offer:

Depending upon how desirable your skills are at your new company, you may be in a position to negotiate more perks or sign-on bonuses at your new job. However, if you are the one reaching out to apply for an open job, you have less negotiating power.

Most employers will ask you what your current salary is. Be honest, but tell them the range you are looking for. Do your homework first—you need to ensure you are competitive with the marketplace—and give a reason why you deserve to be paid more than you are now. For example, do you have new skills or education that you have not been compensated for at your current job?

If you are in a position to negotiate, calculate what you are leaving on the table, especially in terms of forfeited bonus and stock awards, if applicable. Let your potential new employer know that before-tax value. They may offer you stock in the new company with an equal value. The more up-front cash you are asking for as a sign-on bonus, the less likely they'll meet your demands. But stock, since it often has a vesting schedule, tends to be more freely handed out.

It's not common for new employers to compensate you for forfeited 401(k) match or pension credits, but you still need to know this. If the window is open to mention it, address it.

Did you have to sign a non-compete or non-solicit agreement with your prior company? Will you need to do so with your new company? Is there a hold harmless period? Your new employer may not make you sign those agreements until you've been there for six or twelve months, which is ideal. You don't want to lock yourself in somewhere until you know you'll be happy there!

Finally, this is your opportunity to bring your *alpha self*! Don't be afraid to ask for what you want. Speak proudly about your accomplishments, how you can benefit this new company, what unique skills you bring to the table, and how excited you are to be a part of their team.

CHAPTER 7

From Daddy to Husband—Who's Controlling Your Purse Strings?

This chapter was the impetus for writing this book. I was having more and more experiences where female clients were getting divorced and were totally scared out of their minds about money and their financial futures. In one case, a female client was so distrusting of others that she simply dragged her feet and constantly questioned every piece of advice I gave her—no matter how small or obvious.

Money is emotional, and women tend to be more emotional creatures. But when it comes to self-confidence and assurance about your financial future, there is no excuse for taking a back seat. In a 2015 study by Fidelity Investments, 62 percent of women admitted they were at least a little confused about navigating their financial futures and could use more knowledge to make smarter financial decisions. Financial education must start at a young age, and it is a lifelong learning process since the financial world is constantly evolving.

Early in your life, your father may have handled all of your money matters. Even in college, this may have been the case, and he was there to help you get your first job, buy your first car, and rent your first apartment. Sure, there are many activities you enjoyed better, such as social activities or planning your next vacation, so it was easy to let Dad handle the details. By the way, one statistic I heard years ago was that the average person spends more time planning their vacations than planning their finances!

When you get married, your husband or significant other may take over the finances. Easy for you, huh? Think again.

You cannot get lazy or too comfortable allowing someone else—like a father or husband or partner—manage your money. If you idly let someone else control your purse strings, you may get seriously burned. You'll need a major crash course in finances at what could be a very emotional and overwhelming time in your life (death, divorce, legal issue).

Men and Women Approach Money Differently

In my professional experience, I often see men and women approach money from different angles. Men tend to focus more on growing the bottom line and paying less in income taxes. Women are more concerned about financial security, not running out of money, or not having enough resources to provide for the wants and needs of their children.

Women who have been burned before have a higher trust hurdle to overcome. This can be perilous when it comes to finances; if she's not willing to trust the person giving her advice, she'll take little action. With money, some action is often better than no action. These stereotypes are not always the case; they are generalizations of what I've witnessed over the past nearly two decades.

Through your teenage and early college years, you probably went straight to your parents when you needed money or money guidance. You may have found the advice you received from Mom was not exactly the same as Dad. In many households, the financial responsibility is often segregated; one person handles the money and (hopefully) informs the other party. That person may be more knowledgeable about money since they've had to deal with managing the money over the years. It's not always the man who runs the money, but even today, that's the most common scenario I see. (That's not the case though in my house!)

Know Who and What You Are Committing To

If and when you get serious about getting married or forming a long-term union, it's incredibly important to understand your future spouse or significant other's views on money. Did this person grow up privileged? If so, would they be able to cut back and live without all the extras if push came to shove? Can you? Are they debt averse or a speculative investor? Do they budget?

You need to understand where this other person stands financially today. Are you marrying or committing to a mountain of student loans and credit card debt? Are you coming into the relationship on a stronger financial foot? If so, consider a prenuptial agreement. Be sure any inheritance you receive is kept in a bank or brokerage account just in your name since it could be subject to division in the event of a divorce.

Know What You Are Signing

Even if the decision has been made that your spouse or partner is going to primarily be in charge of the finances, here is a list of things you must stay on top of to protect your financial future:

- Tax return. Understand what the numbers mean on your tax return before you sign it. Don't ever let someone force you to sign a joint tax return if you are not comfortable with the numbers, if they are not providing you all the pages in the tax return, or if someone is placing a hand over a section of the page you are supposed to sign. If any of those situations occur, don't sign it!

- Your will. Understand who you are agreeing to give your money to if you were to pass away. Every adult, even those in their twenties, should have a will, a financial power of attorney naming someone to make money decisions for them if they are alive but incapacitated, and a health care power of attorney to make medical decisions for them if they are incapacitated. It is your decision who to name as your agents, your executor, and your beneficiaries. Your will and other legal documents don't need to match your spouse or significant other! If you ever get divorced, you need to update these documents immediately.

- Credit card statement. At a minimum, look at the balance once a month and know if you are paying in full or why you are carrying a balance. Ensure the minimum payments are at least being made. If your name is on that credit account and minimum payments are not being made, your credit score is going down the tubes.

- Have at least two utility bills in your name, which helps your credit score, and ensure they are consistently paid on time.

- Consider having your own bank account, even if it's small, which allows you to have some of your own money, keep using your own debit card, and quick access to cash in an emergency.

- Know your family's professional advisors (financial planner, insurance agent, tax preparer, and attorney) and how to contact them. Sit in on meetings to understand how your financial, tax, or legal plans are progressing. If you don't have professional advisors, review your year-end investment account statements at a minimum and ask to see a copy of your family's balance sheet once a year if your spouse/partner tracks that.

- Be able to access your passport.

- Review your life insurance, disability insurance, and home/auto/liability insurance coverages once a year.

Just spot-check to make sure the total coverage seems reasonable. For example, did your husband drop the $1,000,000 life insurance policy naming you as the beneficiary to $250,000 with your children now named as the beneficiary?

I've Lost Control—How Do I Get it Back without Appearing Suspicious or Mistrusting?

I see many women starting to get more involved in their family finances when they fear something is going wrong—either with the money or with their relationship—especially if they think their spouse is cheating on them. If you haven't been doing the steps I've listed above, how do you start without rocking the boat, perhaps unnecessarily? One idea is to start small.

Begin opening everything that comes in the mail. Stop in at your local bank, sit down with one of the customer service representatives, and ask questions about your accounts, including deposits and withdrawals. Go through your tax-return file since you need a lot of backup documents in order to provide all the inputs necessary to complete the tax return. This will include investment account reports, W-2 wage statements, documents for charitable gifts, property taxes, IRA or 401(k) contributions made to retirement accounts, and bank statements.

Start to pull together your list of questions, do some research, and ask your girlfriends about what they are doing with their finances. Explain that you are trying to get more educated since you realize now is the time to plan for retirement. If you can figure some of it out yourself, you will have fewer questions to ask your spouse or significant other when it's time to confront them. And it may seem less suspicious if you are asking well-informed, educated questions. You may be surprised at how impressed your spouse or partner will be with your proactiveness to educate yourself. It shows that you want to be more involved.

One potential misstep is trying to schedule a meeting with one of your professional advisors without including your spouse or significant other. Many professionals have an obligation to share information with both parties, and they will not conceal information since you are both their client. In fact, if someone is willing to keep your secrets and meet with you separately, they could be doing the same for your spouse or significant other! If you schedule a joint meeting with your advisors, it's a great time to ask your questions. You may find that more information comes out about your finances than you realized by doing your own research. You can also insist they copy you on all correspondence regarding the financial affairs that your professional advisors handle.

If you receive any pushback from your spouse/significant other, it's a sign there is a real problem. You need to confront this right away—and find yourself a good marital lawyer.

Healthy marriages or long-term relationships require communication about money. Be sure that door always stays open for you.

CHAPTER 8

Buying and Filling Your Family Home—Racking Up Big-Time Debt

Prior to this point, buying your first car may have been the biggest purchase of your life. By now, you may have paid off your first car or have a short amount of time left to pay on it. Have you learned any lessons about the amount of money you spent on this car? Was it a good decision? Did you go over the top? Would it have been better to buy something more moderate or have more up-front cash, so you didn't have to borrow as much? Have you wondered why the car dealership suggested you could afford it?

You should use your experience in buying your first car and apply it to the grand purchase you are eyeing now: your first house! It's so important to figure out how much you can afford—or how much you are willing to pay—before you start house shopping since it can be a pretty emotional process. Your eyes will get bigger when you walk into a nicer house, and you'll start rationalizing why you should pay a little more than you planned. Look at what you're getting for your money!

This is where I have seen a lot of my clients get in trouble. Some will ask my advice to determine how much house they can afford, and then they spend 20 percent more than that amount. Buying a house seems like it can be a logical and practical process, but it isn't. You need to keep in mind that the person selling the house has created important memories, so this house is a home to them. It could be the largest investment they've ever made. They're not willing to let you come in and get a steal unless they're selling under extreme duress. You feel so grown-up buying a house, but you are totally inexperienced and appear an easy target to take advantage of. As you can see, lots of emotions are in play.

That's why you need to use your practical head, get a budget in place, and determine your criteria for what, when, where, how, and why you are buying a house *before* you engage a real estate agent and start shopping around. If it's a hot real estate market, someone is going to swoop in and outbid you for the same house. You're going to get frustrated, angry, and overly aggressive with your next offer. Remember that you are buying your first house, and you will likely upgrade in a few years as your career progresses or your family grows, so don't look at it as a forever purchase.

Regardless of advice from parents about how much you should target for your starter home, you are about to saddle yourself with a *big* fixed expense: the mortgage.

Why is separately calculating your fixed expenses and your variable or discretionary expenses important? Because fixed expenses handcuff you more, especially in tough financial times. If you lose your job, you can skip a vacation, but skipping a mortgage payment has severe consequences.

So how much home can you afford? Many financial textbooks will say to limit your debt payments to no more than 25–30 percent of your income. Is that before-tax income or after-tax income? While textbooks will often say "before-tax," I'd argue it should be after-tax income. For example, let's say you make $100,000 in salary. If you target a $2,500/month (or $30,000/year) mortgage payment, after income taxes are taken out of your paycheck, that $30,000 is going to be closer to 40–45 percent of your take-home pay. That's almost half of your paycheck, and it doesn't even factor in groceries, vacations, furnishings, home repairs, a car payment, or student loan debt. In my example, you should target a $1,500–$1,800 monthly mortgage payment to stay in the 25–30 percent after-tax income range. That is a much different price range. On a thirty-year mortgage, targeting a monthly payment based off your take-home pay is the difference of buying a $465,000 house (spending 30 percent of your before-tax pay) versus a $335,000 house (spending 30 percent of your after-tax pay). The banks will probably tell you that you can afford more than this based upon debt-to-income and debt-to-asset ratios. If you have student loans, car payments, or credit card debt, those all count against how much money the bank is willing to lend you, which is another reason to get your ducks in a row before you start house shopping.

Also included in the monthly mortgage payment is money for *escrow*, a monthly reserve for home insurance and real estate taxes. Depending on what part of the country or what town you are buying in, the real estate taxes could be a huge addition to your monthly payment. You need to understand what the real estate taxes are in the area. Are they 1 percent of the home value, 2 percent, or more? Find out from your real estate agent what the current homeowners are paying to insure the house. That could amount to another $100 or $200 per month.

You can decide to pay your insurance and real estate taxes on the house annually, and not escrow monthly, but you will need to ensure you can save enough each month to write those large checks each year. Many first-time homebuyers do not have the extra cash flow to come up with thousands of dollars during the year unless they budget carefully each month to set that money aside.

Finally, it's imperative that you are saving as much cash as you possibly can before you buy this house. The larger the cash down payment, the more home you can afford since you don't have to borrow as much money, which lowers your monthly mortgage payment. The less you borrow, the less the house will cost you over the years. Let's say you are looking to buy a $300,000 house or condo, and you can put 20 percent down ($60,000). Your mortgage payment (excluding taxes and insurance) will be about $1,300/month. Over the span of thirty years with an assumed mortgage interest rate of 5 percent, the total interest expense is almost $225,000, meaning this house will really end up costing you about $525,000.

Let's say you did not do a good job of saving and could only come up with $15,000 to put down (5 percent). Your new mortgage payment will be about $1,525/month. Over the span of thirty years, this same house will cost you a total of $566,000. Doesn't sound like a bargain, does it? The bank may not even allow you to only put down 5 percent without charging you a higher interest rate, having to take out a second mortgage to meet their down payment requirements, or charging PMI. *Personal mortgage insurance* is an extra fee for not having at least 20 percent equity in the house. Equity is the amount the house is worth above the loan amount. For a $300,000 house where you made a 5 percent down payment, the equity in the home is $15,000. If you get a home appraisal a few years later that says your home is worth $310,000, and you owe $279,000, then your equity is $31,000 or 10 percent.

Enough of the numbers—let me boil this experience down by sharing a personal story with you. When I was twenty-five years old, I was dating someone very seriously and had a good idea that we were going to get married one day. We both had full-time jobs, and other than car payments, we had no debt. Being the planner that I am, I decided it was time to buy a house, and my not-yet-husband and I decided to embark on this venture together. (In hindsight, it was not very wise to buy a house with someone I was not at least engaged to yet! Fortunately for us, it worked out and we've been married for fifteen years now.)

We were riding around with our real estate agent and looking at homes, and the farther away from the city we got, the bigger the houses were that fell in our price range. We set an outside boundary and committed to ourselves that we were not going to move beyond that point, especially considering our daily commute to work. Well, lo and behold, we made an offer on a four-bedroom, three-bath house about a quarter mile from our boundary (so much for a decent commute!). The house we made an offer on had a beautiful entryway that looked like a castle. I felt like a princess; I was emotionally hooked.

Against my boyfriend's better judgment, I kept pushing to go in at a higher offer. I was going to be so upset if we didn't get that house. So we did, and then I about lost it when the negotiating process started. I wanted to say yes to all of the seller's demands just so I could have my fairy tale come true (but it was just a house!). We ended up exceeding our budget by $15,000, got the house, and then quickly learned a life lesson when we found out the building material had all these lawsuits against it as water would seep through it and into the house. It was a huge negative when we tried to sell the house, but upgrading it was going to cost at least $10,000—and we were already feeling broke. We had no real furnishings, and many of our rooms sat empty. We even bought some "fancy" white sitting room furniture off a random truck that was driving through our neighborhood one day. It looked so pretty (again playing off my emotions), but once we got it inside the house, I realized it was so uncomfortable!

Because we had tried to put a larger down payment on our first home and then kept bleeding money for random maintenance issues, repairs, and appliances, we really had not rebuilt any savings. I was down to $4,000 in savings when I made a job change that landed me out of work for a few months. We were in big trouble since my husband's paycheck was just barely enough to cover our monthly mortgage—with no food, utilities, or anything else. Fortunately, we stabilized and were able to keep going, but it was a close call.

I learned a few key lessons through my own experience in buying our first home. Never exceed your budget for the purchase price. Don't be afraid to walk away from the house if the negotiations are not in your favor. Be patient during the process. Make sure you can make it on one income if push comes to shove (as you prepare your budget for your house). And never spend every dime you have on the down payment, leaving nothing for the unexpected home expenses. If there's one thing you can bank on as a homeowner, it is the continuous unexpected expenses.

In 2006, we bought our next house, which we've lived in for over a decade, and I implemented these lessons. Knowing I was likely to get emotional again, once we found a house we both liked, I stepped aside and let my husband handle the negotiations. I know that may sound counterintuitive to the whole message of this book, but it's not. It's knowing my strengths and weaknesses and delegating to someone whose strengths balanced out my weaknesses. I stepped back not because I was afraid to negotiate—I just knew we had a higher probability of getting a fair deal if my husband was running the negotiations.

Since we had been saving for the down payment on house #2 and were being conservative with what we thought we could get out of house #1, we built tremendous flexibility for the next time life threw us a curveball. Three months after house #2 was bought, my husband's car died and had to be replaced, adding a $400/month new car payment. Two years after that, we were pregnant with twins and my husband lost his job unexpectedly during the worst financial crisis we've all ever experienced. We were able to weather that storm through savings in the bank—and it came at a time where our family's expenses were about to skyrocket with two babies in diapers. Maintaining some cash savings and building it back up when you must tap into it is a lifelong cycle, yet it's the foundation of your financial security.

My husband and I have moved into a phase where paying off our mortgage is the goal; it's all part of the evolution of you and your money. While paying off your mortgage may seem too distant in the future, I'd like to preview some advice that I often don't need to give clients until they are in their forties or later. Once you are settled in your long-term home, you will want a strategy for paying it off sooner than your mortgage schedule. The endgame is to have one house completely paid for by the time you retire. This keeps your fixed expenses lower in retirement—at a time when you don't have a paycheck coming in and you don't want to be forced to go back to work. It's a huge security blanket to not owe the bank any money on your house. The equity is all yours from thereon out. I've seen some people put all of their savings into paying extra on their mortgage and getting that mortgage done as soon as possible. However, the big problem is that you can't buy groceries with the equity in your house. You still need to be saving cash and have investments built up— liquidity—should you ever need to tap into savings before you retire, and especially after you retire.

I've seen people hammering away at their mortgages because they simply don't know what else to do with their money. They don't know where to save it or how to invest it, and they are either scared to go down that route or are afraid to ask for help. Don't wait to ask for help! While I'm a big advocate of paying down your mortgage and saving on interest expenses, don't sacrifice other parts of your financial plan. You *should* be aggressive in paying down debt if you've racked up large credit card bills. Then, by all means, put both feet on the gas pedal and pay off those credit cards as soon as possible.

CHAPTER 9

Starting Your Family—Get Ready to Spend $1 Million

This wonderful life event is filled with excitement and lots of anxiety for most young women. Becoming a mother may have been a lifelong dream for you. You may have discovered that as a child when you were playing with your baby dolls. Perhaps you treasured the chance to babysit as a teenager, enjoying families with younger children. Those babies were so cute and cuddly! And as a parent, you'll get to experience the love and adoration a child will give to *you*.

As much as you may want to daydream about how your life will change once you have a bundle of joy of your own, this, like many major life events, can go more smoothly if you plan ahead. Over the life of raising a child and sending them to college, parents can easily expect to spend $1.1 million per child (Time.com)!

The expense of having a child begins before they are born. If you are fortunate enough to have good health insurance, delivering a baby may only cost you your annual deductible, which can be as little as $1,000 or $3,000. The actual doctor's bills and hospital bills could run ten times more than that. Be sure you understand how much of your pregnancy and delivery costs your insurance will pick up.

Even before the baby is born, you'll need to spend money to set up the nursery and buy furniture and diapers. There are plenty of items you'll receive at a baby shower, but outside of that, be prepared to spend $1,000 or $2,000 (or more) of your own money to get your housing situation established. If you don't live in a place that has enough space to accommodate another person, then you'll surely have much larger expenses before the baby is born if you need to move into a house or condo or rent a bigger apartment. Don't forget about your car situation. A baby seat must fit in the back seat, so no more cute two-door convertible!

Once your baby arrives, here is a list of necessary items your dollars will be going toward:

- diapers ($60/month)
- formula, if not breastfeeding ($150/month)
- medications, if needed ($50/month or more)
- laundry detergent (you'll do a lot of laundry) ($25/month)
- cleaning supplies ($20/month)
- bath supplies for the baby ($10/month)

- toys (this could get out of control!) ($50/month)
- baby food or the appliances to make your own ($50–$100/month)
- nanny or day care expenses ($1,000/month+)

With all of the above factored in, don't be surprised if you are spending an extra $400/month while you are on maternity leave and an extra $1,500 or more per month if you need to hire a caregiver once you go back to work. According to a USDA study, plan to spend at least $12,500 in the first year of your baby's life.

For the first five years, you should expect to have a lot of financial outlays for your child and their care. It's expensive! You'll have other expenses that are likely decreasing, such as eating out or vacations (you're too tired to travel), so some of this will balance itself out. If you are living on a shoestring budget before your baby is born, you need to make major changes in order to afford to bring a baby into this world.

Not surprisingly, I have many friends who celebrated when they paid their last day care bill and spent their last dollar on diapers. It will feel like a raise! However, according to a recent *Wall Street Journal* article, over the life of your child through age eighteen, it costs an average of $17,000 per year to raise that child.

As your children enter school-aged years, the expenses change. You will be paying for extracurricular activities, more clothing and shoes, school supplies, outings with their friends (or constantly having a friend tag along with you), and perhaps braces. Grocery bills and dining out will become one of the largest categories of expense for you, if they are not already. Feeding one more mouth may not seem like a big difference, but their taste buds are going to be different than yours, and you'll likely not want chicken nuggets for dinner just like they won't want grilled fish and broccoli.

Importantly, if you are not living in a good school district when your child enters kindergarten, you may need to fork over $5,000–$15,000 or more for private school annual tuition. The cost of private school is lower when your child is younger but will increase as they get older.

How do you save any money for your future retirement or your child's future college? You *must* find a way—and don't delay a single year. The power of saving early and saving often is huge, and it's critical to not put yourself in a jam when you are ready to retire.

Take the example of saving for college. A midrange college costs about $40,000 annually. If you have a newborn today, by the time they enter college at age eighteen, the cost could easily be $96,000 per year with a total bill of $400,000! Those eighteen years will fly by, and if you don't sock away some money every single year, the consequences will hit you in the face later in life.

The point of this chapter is to start you thinking through your desire to be a parent while being employed outside the home. It will take more income to raise a family than to just support yourself. As obvious as that may seem, many young women don't give this much thought until they get pregnant.

The sooner you start considering this, the better chance you'll have of maintaining a good quality of life and determining how your job will or will not play a role when you become a mom.

Read on for a major and potentially life-changing decision with large financial impact and personal sacrifices. But first, here is a message about money to new parents.

CHAPTER 10

Money Messages when Raising Kids

New parents, this chapter is for you. From a very young age, children are learning about money. And often at first it's a negative experience. They are told no when they ask for a toy they see on television or a cupcake on display in the grocery store. Why are kids being told they can't have every toy they see? Toys cost money, and family budgets are typically not unlimited when it comes to toys and other discretionary objects. Sure, it warms parents' hearts to give their children gifts, seeing wide grins on their innocent faces, but parents know they must set limits. Children don't understand this at the age of two.

What kids first learn about money comes from watching and listening to their parents. Kids absorb everything parents say and do, and discussing money in front of your kids gives them an early impression about this important part of life.

How often did your parents talk with you about money? In how many subtle ways did money issues circulate your home? Simple day-to-day comments will be absorbed in a child's brain and cause reactions in them: "The water bill was what last month?" "That trip to Disney is costing a fortune!" "We'll never be able to get this house paid off!"

Once kids start to understand "we can't afford that" or "we need to cut back," they start to get a real understanding that money has a major impact on them, but as children, they have no control over it. They are trusting Mom and Dad to handle that well so they can hear the word yes more than they hear the word no. As parents, you are in sole control of the money messages that get ingrained in your children.

One thing I did not experience much of was hearing my parents fight about money. That's rare. How often do you fight with your spouse about money? Kids will pick up on the fact that money is causing marital strain, hindering family harmony, and creating a stressful home environment. That's not what most parents want or plan for when they start a family, but it's life. It's a reality that money does not grow on trees, and to keep the household moving forward, money plays a critical role. It is a natural discussion point. If money is tearing your marriage apart, your children won't forget that—and they could very likely find themselves in a failed marriage too.

When my husband and I were going through our premarital counseling at our church, we were told to sit in separate rooms and answer about fifty questions. I was shocked at how many questions were about money. *Really? Is this what love and marriage are all about?* I was naïve at the time since my parents and my husband's parents had both been married for more than thirty years—the first and only marriage for both of our parents. I never personally knew divorce. However, according to a 2018 survey by Ramsey Solutions, money fights are the second leading cause of divorce (behind infidelity).

How your children experience money growing up, watching and listening to you, can have a lifelong impact on their personal lives. Kids need to have a realistic view of money so that they can grow up having a healthy relationship with money. The healthier this relationship, the more secure your child will likely be as an adult.

Money does make the world go around. Money does impact our happiness. Money will always be a part of your child's life. So be thoughtful about how you teach and show your children the lessons you want them to learn about money.

CHAPTER 11

A Painful Decision—Giving Up your Career for Your Family

I'm forty-one years old at the time I'm writing this book, and I struggle with whether I made the right decision to be a working mom every single day of my life. In truth, while there is a critical time in your life to make this decision—it's often right before or during your maternity leave with your first child—it's a decision most women struggle with for the rest of their lives. Yes, I said rest of their lives.

Early on, the struggle will range from being away from your baby to give a sales presentation, seeing your child cry for your nanny or husband/partner and not for you, or experiencing that disappointment on your child's face when you are the only mom who missed their third-grade musical performance. Then, as the years pass, your child might not come to you with questions or problems because they don't know what time you'll be home from work that night or what day you'll be back from your business trip. They may start spending more time with their friends and not want to be around their parents anymore. You might start regretting all those hours you weren't home to watch them grow up and hug them.

Then, when you are older and retired and possibly have grandchildren, there will certainly be times when you reflect and think about what you could have done better—or differently—and whether you had the influence on the world you wanted to have. Did you impact the people you love positively? Did you spend the right amount of time with your spouse/partner, your kids, and your job? This balance is what "having it all" means to so many women. It's having a happy family life and a fabulous career.

You will likely change your mind a multitude of times about career versus family life for the next eighteen years—or more—when you have children living in your home. Women tend to want it all and think they can have it all. There have been many books written about the ability to have it all. As each day passes, you may totally change your perception of whether you have it all or what you can do differently to have it all. Balancing family and work life is a major challenge. You are trying to balance two incredibly fulfilling and personally defining elements of life.

For a career-oriented young woman, the decision to be a working mom or a stay-at-home mom may be the single largest personal decision you'll ever make. It has massive impact on so many areas of your own life—personal identity, personal happiness, life satisfaction, self-esteem, and a sense of belonging. The emotional tug-of-war between balancing work life and family life pulls at any woman's heart if she needs to be away from her children to earn a paycheck.

If you are fortunate enough to have saved well, have financial support from a family trust or inheritance, or have a spouse with a good-paying job, the choice to become a full-time mother will probably happen as soon as your first child is born. And it's painful. There are so many things you've worked your whole life for that will either be temporarily on hold or lost forever.

This decision has near-term and lifelong implications, including financial ones. So, how do you make this decision? Here is a list of considerations to start with. Be sure your spouse or partner has an equal say in the decision-making process.

Financial

- Do we need my paycheck to make ends meet right now? If so, do we need to downsize into a less expensive house or a less expensive area? This is often difficult to implement since many people having their first child have just bought their first home or condo and are just getting settled. All of the money spent on closing costs and other fees to settle into your first home or condo will have been wasted. And if your house has not appreciated at all, the money you scraped together for the down payment won't be there to make a big down payment on a less expensive house. After all, the goal—if you are considering this—is to have a much smaller mortgage (less in monthly fixed expenses).

- Is our emergency cash fund large enough to cover unexpected home, car, or medical expenses for a period of time? If not, don't stop working until you have this safety net. If you are planning to trim back to one paycheck, try to increase your emergency fund to six to twelve months of normal living expenses.

- Are there large credit card bills that we can't seem to get under control? If so, this is a clear sign you either can't afford to lose a paycheck, or you need to seriously cut back on your lifestyle spending and start penny-pinching on every purchase. Are you willing to make those sacrifices? If you are the one staying at home, you'll likely be the one who is spending the money for the household, and this is going to fall on you.

- Do I have a job where working part-time is an option? And if so, does this even make financial sense if I need to hire a caregiver or pay for day care on the days or hours I am working? Do we have family nearby who can be our child's caretaker for free or very little cost?

- If you plan on leaving the workforce for a few years and then go back, consider this statistic: According to the *Wall Street Journal*, women leaving the workforce to raise children for at least three years make 37 percent less in wages upon reentering the workforce. Do not have a preset expectation that you can go back to work years later and pick up right where you left off. You will very likely need to start back at a much lower-paying position and work your way back up. Your educational degrees may not provide that leg up in applying for a job, and your lack of recent work experience will be noticed by future potential employers.

- The longer you are out of the workforce, the greater the impact on your future financial well-being. Retirement will likely be delayed or be less flush than you would desire. Each year you are not adding to retirement savings can equal multiple years that you need to work before you can afford to retire. For example, if you are saving $10,000 annually into your 401(k) now, assuming a moderate 6 percent rate of investment return, over a thirty-year period, that can grow to be worth over $800,000 by the time you retire. Conversely, if you stop saving for ten years, start back up ten years from now, and therefore only have twenty years that you sock away this same $10,000, your nest egg will be cut in half, worth less than $400,000 by the time you want to retire. To play catch-up, you'll need to save a lot more money ($22,000 annually for twenty years versus $10,000 for thirty years) or be more aggressive with the way you invest and earn (13 percent annually versus 6 percent in my thirty-year example). Keep in mind that saving $10,000 annually is most likely well below what a person really needs to save for a comfortable retirement, and future investment returns are unknown and not guaranteed, so ongoing monitoring of your financial plan is critical. To put retirement savings into perspective, in order to pay yourself a salary of $100,000 annually in retirement, you need an investment portfolio of about $2.5 million.

- There is also an ugly and scary reality that faces women who don't have their own money or don't make their own living. The reality is many women stay in bad or even abusive marriages longer when they don't have enough financial resources or career ability to make it on their own. According to the National Domestic Abuse Hotline, one of the top ten reasons women stay in abusive relationships is lack of money or resources: "Financial abuse is common, and a victim may be financially dependent on their abusive partner. Without money, access to resources or even a place to go, it can seem impossible for them to leave the relationship." Hopefully this never happens to you, but it's important to know the unfortunate curveballs life throws at some women. By informing yourself with the knowledge in this book, money won't be a reason you feel stuck in a bad relationship.

Emotional

- Is your job a major part of your identity? Are you ready to answer the question, "So what do you do?" with "I'm a mom"? In today's society, it's not frowned upon for a woman to leave her career behind and run the household, but the higher up the career ladder you've made it, the harder it could be to distance yourself from that identity.

- Will you be fulfilled? What will give you a sense of accomplishment outside of your career? Being a full-time mom and wife can be a thankless job. Do you need recognition? If so, how will you seek this out? Volunteering can fill some of this need for recognition or accomplishment.

- Will you be more self-conscious of your appearance and body image? If you are used to stepping out in style each morning or getting in a great workout several days a week, it's not likely you can keep that up if you are running from dirty diapers to spilled bottles to Cheerios in your hair. If you become less attractive to yourself, your spouse or partner may start to find you less attractive as well. Will their eye stray if you are not keeping up appearances? This should be discussed openly with your spouse or life partner—and not just once—to ensure you are both keeping up your end of the bargain to fulfill one another physically and emotionally.

- Although this is somewhat related to money, will you be okay asking your spouse or partner for money when you have a personal expense? Will it anger you if your spending habits are criticized or watched more closely since there is only one income coming in? Your voice in spending decisions could take a back seat since you are not adding to the bank account each month. How will you handle possibly being treated with less respect if you add nothing new to the family's financial well-being anymore?

The choice of working versus putting my children first is one I have struggled with, and the internal battle continues at times. I've viewed this choice as either taking all that I've learned to build a life for myself and my family or closing that door to fully serve my family. It's about giving up my job, my career prospects, my major identity, and very likely my financial freedom.

I knew heading into parenthood that we could not afford to live on my husband's engineering income alone and still have the comfortable lifestyle in a nice home that I desired for my family. My career had greater earning potential than my husband's career, so I did not truly have a viable choice to give that up for our family.

As mentioned earlier, about two weeks before our twins were born, my husband lost his job. The economy had just sunk, and unemployment was high. Although that was a shock, it came at what we viewed as the worst possible time. We were about to have double the amount of mouths to feed and I realized I did not want that stress in my future. I did not want our family's financial safety to rest on one employer or one person. Having two jobs spread out the risk. Also, I really liked my job as a financial advisor. I loved the sense of accomplishment that came with helping people, the thanks I received from my clients, and the respect I was earning more and more at my company.

I've always been driven, and I did not believe I'd be as personally fulfilled being a full-time mom. In fact, our life story took a major turn when we found out we were pregnant with our third child. My career had progressed to a point where we could seriously consider what to do about my husband's working situation. Should we continue with two careers, hire a nanny for the baby, and still pay for our twins to remain in full day preschool—or should my husband become the "nanny" and move our twins into part-time preschool? We chose the latter, and my husband quit his job after taking twelve weeks of parental leave to ensure he and I would both be happy with him being at home.

I'd say 90 percent of our arrangement has worked out great. I saw an immediate improvement in our twins' relationship with their dad since he was home all the time (he traveled a lot for work before), and I experienced a huge stress reliever since I no longer needed to worry about how to juggle my 8am client meeting if my child was throwing up the night before.

I've been able to put my career on the front burner and even have time to write this book, but the other 10 percent still pulls at me. It's not being there as much as my husband is to experience every little precious moment with our children. In the first few months he was a full-time dad, our four-month-old baby was crying and could only be calmed down if Daddy was holding her. I internalized that as I gave up the bond between mother and child, and it broke me. In fact, I was crying alone in my bedroom closet for an hour before I could calm myself down—and I'm not a crier! I still get jealous of him at times, and it still makes me sick to miss any functions at my children's school where other parents are in attendance, but I'm also a realist and understand I can't have it all.

Early on as a mom, someone said, "I don't want a stranger raising my kids." What she was referring to was having her child spend the majority of their day with a nanny or day care provider instead of the parent. That resonated with me, and it is a big reason why we now have a full-time parent at home— even though our kids are all in elementary school now.

Whatever decision you make should be made based on what is best for you and for your family—and not on what stereotypes dictate.

CHAPTER 12

Losing a Spouse or Partner

I hope you don't experience anything like this for many years, but it's a reality we'll all face one day.

This emotionally devastating life event is where, as a financial advisor, I've seen the wheels fall off the bus for many women. I have sat across the table from women who were suddenly single due to divorce or the death of a spouse, and they were totally overwhelmed with the concept of money.

The driving reason for this book was the frustration I felt seeing many of these women struggling to come to a decision—any decision—about their money once it became their sole responsibility. Even with my financial guidance, the fear they felt about making the wrong decision and having nobody to catch them if they fell, per se, precluded them from moving forward with their money. Every day that went by was going to cost them hundreds—if not thousands—of dollars of wasted financial opportunities from paying interest on credit cards because they were afraid to release the cash in their bank, or sitting on piles of cash from life insurance money and not investing any of it to combat inflation.

One common trait of these women is that they went from Daddy handling their money to husband being in charge. Even when they did work between college and marriage, they either did not do much with their money, like investing in a 401(k) plan, or they spent it all so there were few long-term financial decisions to be made. They gave up the reins to their husbands when they got married, and they chose to not be informed, ask questions, or partake in financial decisions while they were living with someone else who could handle it.

Life is busy, and I truly understand the need for the division of household responsibilities. My husband plays the stereotypical female role where he has less awareness of our financial situation, but he knows who to call for trustworthy guidance if something happens to me. He's had his own bank account, car payment, and credit card, and he was fifty-fifty in the purchase of both of our homes. Those life events, even if seldom, are still important for everyone to have a basic understanding of finances.

Now, while you may be too young to experience losing your spouse or partner, I am previewing this situation so you understand the need to wisely and independently stay on top of your finances. If you do experience this unfortunate life event, you should be equipped to get through it with less stress and more confidence—and hopefully without skipping a beat in your financial life. It might also allow you to escape a bad relationship years before you otherwise would, and on your terms, if money is not the driving concern. Statistics show that nearly half of all marriages fail, and the #2 reason is because of money (marriage.com).

I plan to continue my advice in a subsequent book for women ages thirty to fifty, and at that time, talking about divorce and death is more commonplace than the targeted readership of this book. I hope you don't need to read my second book from cover to cover. If you follow my guidance here, you will have already built your financial foundation.

CHAPTER 13

Top Twelve Financial Moves for All Young Women—Creating Your Financial Plan

The final piece of my financial book for young women in their twenties and thirties is a twelve-step financial action plan, which I often share with the adult children of my clients as a complimentary service. This advice could cost a young woman hundreds or thousands of dollars if she hired a professional financial planner to guide her as she seeks financial advice.

1. Cash on hand. Keep three to six months of living expenses in cash in the bank. Invest excess cash from time to time—unless you have a larger purchase coming up like a home or a new car.

2. Cash flow. Always spend less than you make! With a disciplined savings approach, great wealth can be created over time. How much you save

will likely have a greater impact than how well your investments perform over time.

3. Roth IRA. Target maximum funding for each year ($6,000 in 2019). Consider an S&P 500 Index fund or target retirement date fund. Many mutual fund companies offer these. Make sure you have a beneficiary on file (i.e. spouse, parent, or sibling). You must have at least $6,000 of wages in order to fund the Roth IRA and make less than the IRS stated income limits (single filer, making less than $122,000 in 2019).

4. 401(k). Every time you get a raise, increase your contribution percentage. Strive to maximum fund this account over time at $19,000/year (2019 limit). Make sure you have a beneficiary on file. A good start is to select a target retirement date fund if that is an option or an S&P 500 Index fund. If there is an auto-rebalance feature, elect that option for annual rebalancing.

5. Debt. Pay off any outstanding debt and avoid future debt (other than a reasonable mortgage for your first home).

6. First home. Don't buy a lot more than you can afford at that time. As your situation changes, your housing needs and price tag can change accordingly.

7. Life insurance. Outside of what you may be provided at work, more may be needed once

you get married and especially before you have children. Make sure you have a beneficiary on file with the insurance company (insurance through work or outside of work).

8. Disability insurance. In many cases, taking the maximum group disability insurance offered at your job is prudent, and if desired, you can supplement it with a small policy outside of work. It's a good thing, from a tax perspective, if your disability premiums come out of your paycheck on an after-tax basis.

9. Home/auto/liability insurance. Have a $1 million umbrella policy in place when you buy a home—even if your assets are less than $1 million. Every few years, shop your home and auto insurance to be sure they remain competitive. If you rent now, keep high liability limits on your renter's insurance and car insurance.

10. Estate planning. Have a will and financial and health care powers of attorney in place, and have them updated by an attorney every five or ten years, or as your personal situation changes such as starting a family or moving to a new state.

11. Prenuptial agreement. If you plan to get married, this may be a consideration. Typically, when one person is in a significantly better financial position than the other, a prenuptial agreement is a good

idea. However, if both individuals are in similar financial situations, it may not be necessary.

12. Inheritance received should be kept separate (i.e. a bank or brokerage account in your name) from marital accounts (i.e. a joint bank or brokerage account).

ABOUT THE AUTHOR

Lisa Brown is a partner and wealth advisor at Brightworth in Atlanta, Georgia, a nationally recognized wealth management firm specializing in high net worth clients. Although Brown's clients are affluent, her own upbringing was far more modest. Raised by two schoolteachers in a rural farming town in upstate New York, Brown learned at the age of twelve how hard work translated into money, rising at six o'clock in the morning during her summer breaks to pick strawberries on a farm for twenty-five cents per quart. This perspective laid the foundation for the appreciation she has for money today.

Brown's childhood experience is at the opposite end of the financial spectrum from her professional experience. Over the years, she has been alarmed and frustrated by the number of single women approaching her for financial advice who shared the same unsettling characteristic: a lack self-confidence when it came to making money decisions. These women have relied on their fathers or husbands/partners to handle money matters throughout their lives, taking a back seat to this critical part of their world, and then suddenly found themselves on their own. Scared.

Lisa has taken two decades of experience in the financial services business to teach real-life money lessons to young women in her first book. Her motivation was to educate women at an earlier age to take control of their finances, be prepared, and make wise decisions with their money that will have a profound effect on their entire lives.

Brown's financial advice has been featured in the *New York Times*, the *Wall Street Journal*, CNBC.com, and Yahoo! Finance, and she is a regular columnist for Kiplinger's wealth-creation website. In 2015, Brown was named one of the ten young advisors under the age of 40 to watch by *Financial Advisor* magazine. She lives in the suburbs of Atlanta with her husband and three children.

Printed in the United States
By Bookmasters